ENGLISH PHRASAL VERBS
BOOK 4

3 WORDS A DAY

KEITH S. FOLSE

KELLY SIPPELL

WAYZGOOSE PRESS

English Phrasal Verbs Book 4. 3 Words a Day

Keith S. Folse, Ph.D., Kelly Sippell

Edited by Dorothy Zemach

Cover design by getcovers.com

Printed in the United States

CONTENTS

LIST OF VERBS

PHRASAL VERBS IN BOOK 4 (BY LESSON)

Lesson 1: sit up; start out; turn down

Lesson 2:back up; call out; get in

Lesson 3:blow up; put back; send out

Lesson 4:carry on; run out; set off

Lesson 5:keep on; make out; shut up

Lesson 6:bring about; step back; turn off

Lesson 7:come along; lay down; stand out

Lesson 8:bring down; go around; play out

Lesson 9:break out; get through; hold back

Lesson 10:move back; walk out; write down

PHRASAL VERBS IN BOOK 4 (ALPHABETICAL)

Lesson numbers in parentheses represent the first use of a phrasal verb: (2)

Lesson numbers in brackets represent a recycled phrasal verb: [10]

back up (2)

blow up (3)

break out (9)

bring about (6)

bring down (8) [10]

call out (2) [7]

carry on (4)

come along (7) [8]

get in (2) [4, 8]

get through (9)

go around (8) [9]

hold back (9) [10]

keep on (5) [6]

lay down (7) [8]

make out (5)

move back (10)

play out (8) [9]

put back (3) [4, 5]

run out (4) [6, 7, 10]

send out (3) [5]

set off (4) [9]

shut up (5)

sit up (1) [2]

stand out (7)

start out (1) [2, 3, 6, 9]

step back (6)

turn down (1) [2, 3, 4, 7]

turn off (6)

walk out (10)

write down (10)

INTRODUCTION

Phrasal verbs are one of the most difficult parts of English. They cause headaches for English learners no matter what your first language is. This book will help you with the phrasal verbs that are most frequent in spoken English.

To function well in a new language, you need vocabulary—and lots of it! Some studies say you can do simple things with just 1,000 words, but you can't really speak any language with just 1,000 words. Other experts have said you need 5,000 words, and some recent studies now say you need 10,000 (or even more!) words to speak your new language well. The more vocabulary you have in a new language, the better your speaking and listening will be.

A **phrasal verb** is one type of vocabulary. It consists of a verb and a preposition. The verb is usually a very simple short word like *get, make,* or *take*. The most common prepositions in phrasal verbs (in order of frequency) include *out, in, up, down, on, off, back,* and *over* (Gardner and Davies, 2007).

The problem for English learners is that these two words together have **a new meaning that is not the same as the meaning of just the verb or the meaning of just the preposition**. If you know the meaning of the verb and the meaning of the preposition, it does not mean you know the meaning of the phrasal verb. The meanings are often very different.

For example, let's look at the phrasal verb *call off. Call* mostly means to contact someone on the phone, and *off* is the opposite of *on.* But *call off* means *cancel* and has no connection to a phone: *The coach called off the game.* Other examples include *figure out, go on,* and *show up.*

Learning phrasal verbs is very difficult. English has hundreds of phrasal verbs, and each phrasal verb can have several meanings. In fact, frequently used phrasal verbs can have more than five different meanings.

WHY ARE THE 150 PHRASAL VERBS IN THESE BOOKS IMPORTANT?

You can easily find a list of phrasal verbs on the internet, but those are just lists taken from big dictionaries. Many of those phrasal verbs are not so common, which makes them a waste of your time, and your time is important.

In these five books about phrasal verbs, you will practice the 150 most frequently used phrasal verbs in English. This list is the result of an extensive computer analysis of a large collection of approximately 130 million words of spoken English (PHaVE List: Garnier and Schmitt, 2015).

Sometimes one phrasal verb can have five or more meanings, so what should you learn first? You should learn the most common meanings, so the books in this series teach only the top meanings of each phrasal verb based on important information from a very detailed study by Liu and Myers (2020). The meanings are listed **in order of frequency**, so the first meaning is more frequently used than the second meaning, etc. (A few changes from the original list have been made for better learning.)

In sum, these books teach the most common phrasal verbs with the most common meanings in spoken English. Information about the 150 verbs chosen for these books comes from these sources:

Adolphs, Svenja, and Dawn Knight. "Building a spoken corpus." *The Routledge handbook of corpus linguistics* (2010): 38–52.

Davies, Mark. *The corpus of contemporary American English (COCA).* (2008-): available online at https://www.english-corpora.org/coca/.

Gardner, Dee, and Mark Davies. "Pointing out frequent phrasal verbs: A corpus-based analysis." *TESOL Quarterly* 41.2 (2007): 339–359.

Garnier, Mélodie, and Norbert Schmitt. "The PHaVE List: A pedagogical list of phrasal verbs and their most frequent meaning senses." *Language Teaching Research* 19.6 (2015): 645–666.

Garnier, Mélodie, and Norbert Schmitt. "Picking up polysemous phrasal verbs: How many do learners know and what facilitates this knowledge?" *System* 59 (2016): 29–44.

Liu, Dilin. "The most frequently used English phrasal verbs in American and British English: A multicorpus examination." *TESOL Quarterly* 45.4 (2011): 661–688.

Liu, Dilin, and Daniel Myers. "The most-common phrasal verbs with their key meanings for spoken and academic written English: A corpus analysis." *Language Teaching Research* 24.3 (2020): 403–424.

HOW ARE THESE BOOKS ORGANIZED?

There are five books. The phrasal verbs in Book 1 are more common than those in Book 2, etc., so you should start with Book 1 and continue through the books in order: 2, 3, 4, 5. The order is based on an analysis of millions of words of real English.

Each book has 10 lessons. Each lesson has 3 phrasal verbs. That lesson will focus on those 3 phrasal verbs, but it will also review some of the phrasal verbs from earlier lessons, so you should also do the lessons in order.

Each lesson has these **6 practice activities with some online exercises:**

- Activity 1: CONVERSATION PRACTICE
- Activity 2: LEARNING NEW PHRASAL VERBS
- Activity 3: PRACTICING IMPORTANT PHRASES
- Activity 4: USING CORRECT PREPOSITIONS

- Activity 5: VERBS IN CONTEXT
- Activity 6: ONLINE PRACTICE (with a link allowing for at least 5 different kinds of online practice, including one for instruction)

PRACTICAL ADVICE FOR LEARNING VOCABULARY

You need a lot of vocabulary, and no one can learn this vocabulary for you. A good teacher and a good book can help, but in the end, it's all up to you.

To get more vocabulary, you need to read things in English that interest you. You need to practice speaking in English. You should try to find a conversation partner who can help you practice your lessons of three English phrasal verbs.

Keep a vocabulary notebook, either a traditional paper notebook or an electronic notebook. Every time you see a new English word, write it down. Ask yourself, "Is this word important for me in my English?" If the answer is yes, then ask, "How is this word used?" If the answer is no, then skip it and keep looking for another word.

To remember a new word, look at it carefully. Ask yourself, "Is there anything different or special about the word that can help me remember it? Is the spelling unusual or new to me? Is the word really long? Does it have any double letters?"

Examples:

- VALLEY: You can remember the word *valley* because

it begins with the letter V and a valley is shaped like the letter V.

- ENVELOPE: You can remember the word *envelope* because it starts with *e* and ends with *e*, and not many words in English start and end with the letter *e*.
- MUSTARD: A personal example is the word *mustard*. I like mustard a lot, so I know I need that word when I order a sandwich at a restaurant. If I don't know this word, then I should look for that word in a dictionary and then think of something to help me remember it. To do this well, I am going to imagine a big yellow **M** on top of my sandwich, representing mustard. Whenever you find a new word, try to find something that makes that word different or special to you personally.
- DOZEN: Every time you see a new word that you think is useful for your English purposes, you should stop and make a short example in your head. If the word is *dozen*, then say to yourself, "one dozen eggs, one dozen pencils, one dozen sandwiches." It's okay to practice English with yourself in your own head. This is in fact very good practice. Use the new word and then talk to yourself (silently). It can be something as simple as "I would like some mustard, please." Yes, practice English with yourself by making a short example with each new word.

8 SUGGESTIONS FOR USING THIS BOOK

1. Open the book! Do the lessons! Many students buy a new book but do not complete the book. This book

has only 10 lessons, and each lesson is short. Make time to read the book.

2. Do all the exercises. Even if an exercise seems easy, do it. The more times your brain "touches" each phrasal verb, the better your English vocabulary will become.

3. Each lesson teaches you only 3 phrasal verbs, but these verbs can have several meanings. In fact, some have two meanings, but others have five. Everyone learns differently. Some people can do one lesson in one day, but most people will need a few days with each lesson, so work hard and try to learn these very common, very useful phrasal verbs.

4. When you learn a new phrasal verb, try to learn a very short phrase with the verb. For example, when you learn FIND OUT, you should learn FIND OUT THE ANSWER or FIND OUT HER PHONE NUMBER. When you learn SET UP, you should try to remember SET UP AN APPOINTMENT or SET UP A MEETING.

5. Translations are very good when you first learn a new phrasal verb, but a translation is not your final goal. Your goal is to understand and use the phrasal verb. After you have a clear translation, then make sure you do Step 4: Learn a short phrase with the verb.

6. Every time you see a new phrasal verb, immediately try to make a personal example in your head. For example, when you learn PICK UP, ask yourself, "How can I make an example with PICK UP about my life now?" Maybe you will say, "I need to PICK UP my friend at the airport tonight" or "Please PICK UP the baby." Say this example in your head. Write it

down. It is much better if you practice your new phrasal verb in your head before you try to use it in real conversation.

7. Try to use your new vocabulary in your conversations in English. If you have a conversation partner, share your list of 3 phrasal verbs from your lesson and tell your partner that the goal is to use these 3 phrasal verbs as much as possible in your conversation.

8. This book has many examples and exercises for each phrasal verb, but some people can remember vocabulary better if they can watch a lesson about it from a teacher. One good place to find free and easy-to-access lessons about phrasal verbs is YouTube. For example, if your new phrasal verb is *call off*, just search for "phrasal verb call off" and you will find many short lessons. Some videos are better than others, so if you find a teacher you like, then for the second phrasal verb, see if that same teacher also has a YouTube video lesson about other phrasal verbs.

9. Finally, try to use the phrasal verbs you learned in Books 1, 2, and 3. The more you practice all of these verbs, the better your English will be.

10. Do not worry about mistakes. Remember: Practice makes perfect, so practice, practice, practice!

Good luck learning lots of English vocabulary!

Keith S. Folse and Kelly Sippell

LESSON 1

SIT UP; START OUT; TURN DOWN

ACTIVITY 1: CONVERSATION PRACTICE

A new puppy!

Read this conversation. Think about the meanings of the **3 new bold verbs**. Then answer the comprehension questions.

Leo: Hey, Justin, who is this with you?

Justin: Leo, meet my new puppy, Buddy!

Leo: Well, hello, Buddy! You're so cute!

Justin: Yeah, when I saw him at the animal shelter, I fell in love.

Leo: When did you get him?

Justin: About three months ago. Buddy's a lot of fun, but I forgot how much energy puppies have.

Leo: Have you started training him yet?

Justin: Yes. His first class was exactly a month ago. He **started out** with only one class per week, but I think he might need more hours per week.

Leo: Well, it all sounds good.

Justin: Yes, it is. Last week they tried to teach him to **sit up**, but sometimes he still wants to jump instead.

Leo: You know, I've thought about getting a dog, but I worry about not having enough time for one.

Justin: Yeah, there's a lot to consider. It's certainly more work, but Buddy's good company. And some mornings—like yesterday, when it was raining so hard —I didn't want to go out, but I had to take Buddy outside.

Leo: I was thinking about getting an older dog.

Justin: That's a good idea! When you go to the animal shelter, you'll have a lot of choices. There are always a lot of older dogs there.

Leo: I know. But I'm worried that if I go there, I'll want to leave with a dog, and I'm still not 100% sure I'm ready. It would be hard to **turn** the shelter **down**, but I'm not sure I'm really ready to take care of a dog.

Justin: Well, you'll know when the time is right for you to get a dog. Okay, we need to finish our run and get back home so I won't be late for work. Good to see you!

Leo: Okay. Nice meeting you, Buddy! I hope I see you guys again soon.

1. Where did Justin get Buddy?

   a. at an animal shelter
   b. at a dog training class
   c. in the park

2. What is Buddy learning to do?

   a. sit up
   b. run
   c. jump

3. What does Justin like about having a dog?

   a. Buddy has a lot of energy.
   b. Buddy is good company.
   c. Buddy likes to stay inside when it rains.

4. What doesn't Justin like sometimes about having a dog?

   a. Buddy likes to stay inside when it rains.
   b. Buddy isn't good company.

c. Buddy has a lot of energy at times.

5. Will Leo get a dog?

   a. Yes, he will get a dog in the next few weeks.
   b. No, he will not get a dog because he doesn't like dogs.
   c. He might get an older dog when the time is right for him.

6. How do Justin and Leo know each other?

   a. They work together.
   b. They went to the same college.
   c. We do not know from this conversation.

∾

ACTIVITY 2: LEARNING NEW PHRASAL VERBS

Read this information about 3 phrasal verbs. Study the example sentences carefully. To help learn them, read the example sentences aloud or write them on a sheet of paper or in a document.

#91: SIT UP

91: rise from a lying position to a sitting position; sit with your back straight up (against the back of the chair, for example)

- My grandmother always told me to **sit up** straight in my chair.
- When I heard the nurse open my door, I immediately **sat up** in bed.

#92: START OUT

92: begin a life, profession, or a plan of action by doing a particular thing

- A good number of university professors **start out** as high school teachers.
- Matt **started out** going for a walk only on Mondays, but now he goes for a walk every day.

#93: TURN DOWN

93A: lower the volume or sound

- Can you please **turn down** the TV?
- How do you **turn down** the volume on this device?

93B: say no to an invitation or a request

- Do you think your boss will **turn down** your request for a raise?
- We invited 80 people to the party, and only four or five **turned down** our invitation.

∾

ACTIVITY 3: PRACTICING IMPORTANT PHRASES

Give the phrasal verb for the meaning. Be sure to use the correct verb tense.

1. say no to a job offer = _____ _____ a job offer
2. the doctor told me to sit with my back straight = the doctor told me to_____ _____
3. the game began great = the game _____ _____ great
4. lower the volume of the radio = _____ _____ the radio
5. begin by introducing yourself = _____ _____ by introducing yourself

~

ACTIVITY 4: USING CORRECT PREPOSITIONS

Read the sentences carefully and add the missing prepositions for each phrasal verb.

1. The teacher **started** _____ speaking Spanish and then changed to English.
2. When my dog heard the doorbell ring, she **sat** _____ immediately.
3. Please **turn** _____ the TV. It's too loud!
4. After his surgery, it was hard for Kevin to **sit** _____ for long periods of time.
5. Good luck with your presentation tomorrow. If you **start** _____ well, I'm sure you will finish well.
6. How can you possibly **turn** _____ that job offer?

ACTIVITY 5: VERBS IN CONTEXT

Use the context to select the correct verb for the sentence.

1. How can I (sit up, start out, turn down) my ringtone?
2. I am the owner of this restaurant now, but I (sat up, started out, turned down) here working as a waiter.
3. When the boss came into the meeting, everyone immediately (sat up, started out, turned down) and gave her their full attention.
4. In the soccer match, things (sat up, started out, turned down) slowly, but it got more exciting in the second half.
5. I can't believe you are going to (sit up, start out, turn down) a trip to Europe.

ACTIVITY 6: ONLINE PRACTICE

You can practice the phrasal verbs from this lesson at

https://bit.ly/4kboy6w

Here you can use *Flashcards*, *Learn*, or *Match*. You can also have more guided practice with *Q-Chat* that offers *Teach me*, *Quiz me*, and *Apply my knowledge*.

Answers for Lesson 1

Activity 1

1. a
2. a
3. b
4. c
5. c
6. c

Activity 3

1. turn down
2. sit up
3. started out
4. turn down
5. start out

Activity 4

1. out
2. up
3. down
4. up
5. out
6. down

Activity 5

1. turn down
2. started out
3. sat up
4. started out
5. turn down

LESSON 2

BACK UP; CALL OUT; GET IN

ACTIVITY 1: CONVERSATION PRACTICE

Learning to drive

Read this conversation. Think about the meanings of the **3 new bold verbs**. Remember the meanings of the <u>underlined verbs</u> from earlier lessons. Then answer the comprehension questions.

Dad: Jeff, are you ready now?

Jeff: Ready for what?

Dad: Well, I have some time now. Why don't you **get in** the car so we can practice your driving?

Jeff: Oh, that would be great! My driver's license test is in about two months.

(*They get in the car.*)

Dad: Now, Jeff, what's first? Before you **back up,** what's the first thing you need to do?

Jeff: Put my seat belt on. I know that now because you always **call** me **out** for forgetting to do that.

Dad: Yes, seatbelts are important. Ok, what else?

Jeff: I need to adjust the mirrors.

Dad: Yes, and be sure you are <u>sitting up</u> straight when you do that.

Jeff: Ready? I'm going to start the car now. Then I'll check my mirrors again and, if it's all clear, I'll start **backing up.**

Dad: Good. But would you <u>turn down</u> the radio so you can concentrate on your driving? Okay, let's <u>start out</u> on our street and then go downtown. I think we should practice parking today.

Jeff: That sounds good. I need more practice before I take test. That's for sure. When are we going to go on a highway? That worries me.

Dad: If things go well and we have time, maybe we'll

go on the highway today. But first, let's just drive around town and work on turns and parking. Why don't you turn left on Elm Street? Let's go to the post office. Parking there can be a little difficult. Some of those spaces are hard to **get into.**

Jeff: Yeah, people are always pulling out of parking spaces without looking. And some people park illegally.

Dad: Yes. That's why we're going to go there first. Then we'll work on turns and changing lanes. If there isn't too much traffic and I still have time, we can go on the highway.

Jeff: Okay. I'm really glad you had time today to help me get my license.

1. Why is Jeff in the car?

   a. He is going to the post office to mail something.
   b. He is checking his mirrors.
   c. He is practicing for his driver's test.

2. What does Jeff do first when he gets in the car?

   a. starts the car
   b. puts on his seatbelt
   c. adjusts the mirrors

3. How much time does Jeff have to practice for this test?

   a. two months
   b. two weeks

c. two days

4. Where are Jeff and his dad going first?

    a. on the highway
    b. to take the driver's test
    c. to the post office parking lot

5. Which of these is NOT a problem with parking at the post office?

    a. People park illegally.
    b. There are not enough parking spaces.
    c. The spaces are hard to get into.

6. Will Jeff practice driving on the highway today?

    a. yes
    b. no
    c. maybe

~

ACTIVITY 2: LEARNING NEW PHRASAL VERBS

Read this information about 3 phrasal verbs. Study the example sentences carefully. To help learn them, read the example sentences aloud or write them on a sheet of paper or in a document.

#94: BACK UP

94A: make a copy of a computer file or similar to save the information

- For each assignment, I **back up** that file at the end of every day.
- Before the storm comes, you might want to **back up** your computer in case we lose power.

94B: move or drive backward a short distance

- If the driver of the white car **backs up** just a little, I think I can park in that space.
- The gate agent asked the customers in line to **back up** so a woman in a wheelchair could get by.

94C: support or provide support

- Good writers **back up** their big ideas with data that proves their point.
- In the meeting tomorrow, I'm going to ask our boss for a raise for our group, and I hope you can **back** me **up** if he has any questions.

#95: CALL OUT

95A: speak or say loudly or excitedly

- If you work in a busy coffee shop, you need a strong voice to be able to **call out** customers' names all day long.
- She **called out** "Bingo" when she had five in a row on her card.

95B: criticize publicly

- The website host **called out** people who were not following the rules about commenting on the site.
- The teacher **called out** two students who were cheating on the exam.

#96: GET IN(TO)

96: enter a car, a place, or a situation

- As soon as you **get into** a car, you should check the mirrors.
- Laura applied for admission to the university for several years, and she finally **got in** in 2025.

∾

ACTIVITY 3: PRACTICING IMPORTANT PHRASES

Give the phrasal verb for the meaning. Be sure to use the correct verb tense.

1. say the winner's name loudly = _____ _____ the winner's name
2. enter a taxi = _____ _____ a taxi
3. make a copy of the work on your computer = _____ _____ the work on your computer
4. become part of an argument = _____ _____ an argument
5. support the ideas in your essay = _____ _____ the ideas in your essay

∾

ACTIVITY 4: USING CORRECT PREPOSITIONS

Read the sentences carefully and add the missing prepositions for each phrasal verb.

1. What time did you **get** _____ the office this morning?
2. Could you **back** _____ a little so I can open this closet door?
3. A lifeguard listens for swimmers who might **call** _____ for help.
4. It's not good to **get** _____ a taxi with food or drink.
5. Did you remember to **back** _____ all of the files?
6. I thought I heard someone **call** _____ my name.

∾

ACTIVITY 5: VERBS IN CONTEXT

Use the context to select the correct verb for the sentence.

1. Oh, no! I forgot to (back up, call out, get in) both files before the meeting.
2. I applied for an internship program for three consecutive years, and I finally (backed up, called out, got in) in 2023.
3. If you have a question, just (back up, call out, get in), and I'll come help you.
4. That politician almost never (backs up, calls out, gets in) his statements with any real facts.
5. If you could just (back up, call out, get in) a little, I can open the door more easily.

∼

ACTIVITY 6: ONLINE PRACTICE

You can practice the phrasal verbs from this lesson at

https://bit.ly/433PYoN

Here you can use *Flashcards*, *Learn*, or *Match*. You can also have more guided practice with *Q-Chat* that offers *Teach me*, *Quiz me*, and *Apply my knowledge*.

Answers for Lesson 2

Activity 1

1. c
2. b
3. a
4. c
5. b
6. c

Activity 3

1. call out
2. get in/into
3. back up
4. get in/into
5. back up

Activity 4

1. in/into
2. up
3. out
4. in/into
5. up
6. out

Activity 5

1. back up
2. got in
3. call out
4. backs up
5. back up

LESSON 3
BLOW UP; PUT BACK; SEND OUT

ACTIVITY 1: CONVERSATION PRACTICE

An anniversary party

Read this conversation. Think about the meanings of the **3 new bold verbs**. Remember the meanings of the <u>underlined verbs</u> from earlier lessons. Then answer the comprehension questions.

Vicky: Hey, Paula. Is everything ready for the party?
Paula: Almost. I just finished **blowing up** all the balloons and putting up all the other decorations.
Vicky: Wow, it looks great in here! Good job!
Paula: How does the sign look?
Vicky: I like it!
Paula: Gosh, what time is it?
Vicky: It's almost 5:00. We should let people in.
Paula: Yes, we should. I'm going to **put** my tape and supplies **back** in the drawer and get them out of the way. Then I'll let my sister know that she should bring the cake and the other food out now.
Vicky: Good. Do you know how many people are coming?
Paula: Yes. We **sent out** 50 invitations, and 45 people said they are planning to attend.
Vicky: Wow. That's a great turnout! Hardly anyone <u>turned</u> their invitation <u>down!</u>
Paula: Yes. It's going to be so nice for my parents. They'll be happy that people wanted to celebrate this golden anniversary with them!
Vicky: Well, being married for 50 years is e! I don't know anybody who's been married that long. What is the secret to their success?
Paula: I think my mom would say, "Don't <u>start out</u> thinking about being married for 25 or even 50 years. Just take it one day, and then one year, at a time."
Vicky: That sounds like good advice.
Paula: My parents are also really good friends. I think

that helps, even though I know there were some difficult times too.

Vicky: Of course, but your sister and you are lucky to have them as role models for your marriages.

Paula: Yes, we are.

1. What was Paula doing before 5:00?

    a. putting up decorations and a sign
    b. sending out invitations
    c. making a cake

2. Who is the party for?

    a. Paula and Vicky
    b. Vicky's parents
    c. Paula's parents

3. What is the reason for the party?

    a. celebrating 50 years of marriage
    b. celebrating a young couple's wedding
    c. celebrating a 50th birthday

4. How many people are coming to the party?

    a. 45
    b. 50
    c. We do not know from this conversation.

5. How many brothers and sisters does Paula have?

   a. one
   b. two
   c. We do not know from this conversation.

6. How many years has Paula been married?

   a. 10 years
   b. 25 years
   c. We do not know from this conversation.

∼

ACTIVITY 2: LEARNING NEW PHRASAL VERBS

Read this information about 3 phrasal verbs. Study the example sentences carefully. To help learn them, read the example sentences aloud or write them on a sheet of paper or in a document.

#97: BLOW UP

97A: explode, like a bomb

- Terrorists tried to **blow up** a bridge over the Mississippi River.
- Two soldiers died when the enemy **blew up** their car.

97B: become very angry and react loudly

- I'm sorry I **blew up** at the meeting. I just couldn't keep calm any longer.
- The president **blew up** when the vice president criticized him in public.

97C: cause something to expand by putting air into it

- Look at all these balloons! How long did it take you to **blow** them **up**?
- For camping, I have a special pillow that I have to **blow up**.

#98: PUT BACK

98: move things or people to a place where they were before

- Please **put back** all the files after using them.
- I took out three cans of beans and used only one, so I **put** the others **back**

#99: SEND OUT

99A: distribute something to lots of people

- Our boss **sends out** a weekly memo on Monday mornings.
- I didn't **send out** any emails from this computer today.

99B: order someone or something to a place for a specific reason

- The manager **sent out** the intern to get coffee and pastries for the office.
- The police chief **sent out** officers to every high school in the city.

～

ACTIVITY 3: PRACTICING IMPORTANT PHRASES

Give the phrasal verb for the meaning. Be sure to use the correct verb tense.

1. return the money = _____ the money _____
2. ask Mark to get our lunches = _____ _____ Mark to get our lunches
3. the bomb exploded = the bomb _____ _____
4. place the juice in the refrigerator again = _____ the juice _____ in the refrigerator
5. try not to get very angry = try not to _____ _____

～

ACTIVITY 4: USING CORRECT PREPOSITIONS

Read the sentences carefully and add the missing prepositions for each phrasal verb.

1. Is it true that you can **blow** _____ a potato if you cook it in a microwave for more than ten minutes?
2. How many invitations did they **send** _____?

3. Why is it so hard for you to **put** the milk _____ in the refrigerator after you're done with it?
4. I was going to buy a new shirt and even had it in my hands, but I changed my mind and **put** it _____.
5. The two were put in jail for trying to **blow** _____ an airplane.
6. We were all happy when our boss **sent** two people _____ to get coffee for everyone.

~

ACTIVITY 5: VERBS IN CONTEXT

Use the context to select the correct verb for the sentence.

1. I am sorry that I (blew up, put back, sent out) at you.
2. After you use weights in a gym, you are supposed to (blow them up, put them back, send them out) in the original place.
3. In that TV show, the father always (blows up, puts back, sends out) his dog to get the morning newspaper. Do you think this is possible in real life?
4. Part of my job is to (blow up, put back, send out) emails promoting our company.
5. According to the police report, the bank robbers were planning to (blow up, put back, send out) the bank after they robbed it.

~

ACTIVITY 6: ONLINE PRACTICE

You can practice the phrasal verbs from this lesson at

https://bit.ly/43dhfoL

Here you can use *Flashcards, Learn,* or *Match.* You can also have more guided practice with *Q-Chat* that offers *Teach me, Quiz me,* and *Apply my knowledge.*

Answers for Lesson 3

Activity 1

1. a
2. c
3. a
4. a
5. a
6. c

Activity 3

1. put back
2. send out
3. blew up
4. put back
5. blow up

Activity 4

1. up
2. out
3. back
4. back
5. up
6. out

Activity 5

1. blew up
2. put them back
3. sends out
4. send out
5. blow up

LESSON 4

CARRY ON; RUN OUT; SET OFF

ACTIVITY 1: CONVERSATION PRACTICE

Packing for a trip

Read this conversation. Think about the meanings of the **3 new bold verbs**. Remember the meanings of the underlined verbs from earlier lessons. Then answer the comprehension questions.

Claudia: Jim, do you think we should **set off** for the airport in the next hour?

Jim: Yes, I think so. It looks like your flight is on time, but traffic near the airport is sometimes bad. How much more time do you need to finish packing?

Claudia: Another 30 minutes. I need to figure out which things I'll take on the plane with me and which things I'll put in my checked luggage. I want to make sure I have what I need in case my luggage gets lost.

Jim: Oh, I'm sure that won't happen. But it's good to be prepared.

Claudia: And I need to have a book and some head-phones because it's just too hard to **carry on** a conversation because of the engine noise. I'm so excited about this trip!

Jim: A free place to stay for 2 weeks on Maui! You couldn't turn that down!

Claudia: No way. Now, the question is, how much can I get into this one small bag and my pockets?

Jim: Yeah, and be careful that you don't have anything that could **set off** the metal detectors. That causes such a delay going through security. Last time, you almost missed your flight. Remember?

Claudia: Oh, that's right! Okay, I'll check the size of everything again in case I need to put something back.

Oh, no! It looks like I've **run out of** sunblock, and I'm definitely going to need that in Hawaii!

Jim: Do you want me to **run out** and buy you some more? I can get to the market and get back in about 15 minutes. I can do that while you finish packing.

Claudia: Oh, that would be a big help!

Jim: Okay, I'll be back soon.

1. What is true about Claudia's trip?

   a. She is traveling by train.
   b. She is traveling to Hawaii.
   c. She is traveling with Jim.

2. How many suitcases is Claudia packing?

   a. one
   b. at least two
   c. We don't know from this conversation.

3. What is Claudia worried about?

   a. being too early for her flight
   b. trying to fit everything in both suitcases
   c. losing her luggage

4. What happened the last time Claudia went through airport security?

a. She lost her headphones.

b. She almost missed her flight.

c. She had to repack her suitcase.

5. What happened to the sunblock?

a. Claudia doesn't have any.

b. It was in the luggage that was lost.

c. It was thrown away at the airport.

6. Where is Jim going to go today?

a. to the market

b. to the airport

c. to the market and then to the airport

∿

ACTIVITY 2: LEARNING NEW PHRASAL VERBS

Read this information about 3 phrasal verbs. Study the example sentences carefully. To help learn them, read the example sentences aloud or write them on a sheet of paper or in a document.

#100: CARRY ON

100A: continue to do something, often after something difficult or challenging

- It is important to **carry on** the traditions from one generation to the next.
- We had trouble **carrying on** a conversation because so many babies were crying.

#101: RUN OUT (OF)

101: use completely and have none left

- I think I have enough cash, but if I **run out**, I might use my credit card.
- Unfortunately, we **ran out of** time and couldn't finish the lesson.

#102: SET OFF

102: cause negative things to happen, often with bombs, alarms, or problems

- The person who tried to open the emergency exit **set off** the alarm.
- In the movie, the superhero touched a switch and that **set off** a bomb.

∽

ACTIVITY 3: PRACTICING IMPORTANT PHRASES

Give the phrasal verb for the meaning. Be sure to use the correct verb tense.

1. have no more time = _____ _____ _____ time
2. cause a bomb to explode = _____ _____ a bomb
3. continue without your help = _____ _____ without your help
4. Who caused the alarm to ring? = Who _____ _____ the alarm?
5. spent all the money = _____ _____ _____ money

∾

ACTIVITY 4: USING CORRECT PREPOSITIONS

Read the sentences carefully and add the missing prepositions for each phrasal verb.

1. As soon as she touched the door, it **set** _____ an alarm.
2. I couldn't make more than 20 cookies because I **ran** _____ _____ sugar.
3. I missed the first deadline, and this **set** _____ several other delays on the project.
4. She and I tried to **carry** _____ a conversation, but it was difficult since we spoke different languages.
5. I can't believe I **ran** _____ _____ gas on my way to work.
6. Even though it started to rain harder, we decided to **carry** _____ with our walk.

∾

ACTIVITY 5: VERBS IN CONTEXT

Use the context to select the correct verb for the sentence.

1. Some people have a hard time trying to (carry on, run out, run out of, set off) after the death of a family member.
2. Oh, no! We might (carry on, run out, run out of, set off) water before we finish our hike.
3. The doctor suggested that we (carry on, run out, run out of, set off) with this topic at our next meeting.
4. Unfortunately, we (carried on, ran out, ran out of, set off) Euros before we left Italy.
5. How did someone (carry on, run out, set off) the alarm?

~

ACTIVITY 6: ONLINE PRACTICE

You can practice the phrasal verbs from this lesson at

https://bit.ly/3XgAxFX

Here you can use *Flashcards*, *Learn*, or *Match*. You can also have more guided practice with *Q-Chat* that offers *Teach me*, *Quiz me*, and *Apply my knowledge*.

Answers for Lesson 4

Activity 1

1. b
2. b
3. c
4. b
5. a
6. c

Activity 3

1. run out of
2. set off
3. carry on
4. set off
5. ran out of

Activity 4

1. off
2. out of
3. off
4. on
5. out of
6. on

Activity 5

1. carry on
2. run out of
3. carry on
4. ran out of
5. set him off

LESSON 5

KEEP ON; MAKE OUT; SHUT UP

ACTIVITY 1: CONVERSATION PRACTICE

A bunch of old letters

Read this conversation. Think about the meanings of the **3 new bold verbs**. Remember the meanings of the <u>underlined verbs</u> from earlier lessons. Then answer the comprehension questions.

Brian: Hey Kristen, can you help me **make out** the handwriting on this old letter?

Kristen: Sure, I can try. Wow, that letter is really old. Where did you find it?

Brian: In the attic. I'm helping my mom clean out this cottage this summer so she can sell it.

Kristen: Does she want to sell it soon?

Brian: Well, yes, but we'll wait until next spring. It will sell for a better price then because more people buy cottages in the spring than in the fall or winter.

Kristen: Well, that makes sense. You should have no problem selling it. It's beautiful and quiet here.

Brian: It is, mostly. The neighbor has a dog, though, that just won't **shut up** at night.

Kristen: Well, let's hope it's quiet when people are looking at the house.

Brian: Yeah.

Kristen: Hey, I think I can **make out** who wrote this letter. It looks like it's from your grandfather and was written to your grandmother. Was he a soldier in the war?

Brian: Yes, he was. He was a soldier in Europe.

Kristen: Gosh, it must have been difficult to <u>send out</u> letters in the middle of a war.

Brian: Definitely! It's amazing any letters made it back here. I know it took months for them to arrive.

Kristin: I can't read all of this letter, but it looks like a love letter.

Brian: Really? Cool!

Kristen: Do you think it's the only one, or could there be more?

Brian: I don't know. Let me go downstairs ask my mom if she thinks there could be more letters up here.

Kristen: Okay. I'll **keep on** looking through this old desk and see if I can find anything else interesting. I won't <u>put</u> this letter <u>back</u> in the desk until we know if there might be others.

Brian: Great! That'll be a big help.

1. What does Brian ask Kristen to do?

   a. help him watch something
   b. help him hide something
   c. help him read something

2. What are Brian and Kristen doing?

   a. selling a cottage
   b. cleaning an attic
   c. writing a letter

3. When will the cottage be sold?

   a. in the winter
   b. in the fall
   c. in the spring

4. What are we told about the letter?

   a. It is a love letter.
   b. It is from Brian's grandmother.
   c. It was written after the war.

5. What will happen while Brian is downstairs?

   a. Kristen will continue looking in the desk.
   b. Brian's mom will come to the attic.
   c. We do not know from this conversation.

6. Which war was Brian's grandfather in?

   a. World War 1
   b. World War 2
   c. We do not know from this conversation.

∾

ACTIVITY 2: LEARNING NEW PHRASAL VERBS

Read this information about 3 phrasal verbs. Study the example sentences carefully. To help learn them, read the example sentences aloud or write them on a sheet of paper or in a document.

#103: KEEP ON [+ verb-ing]

103: continue doing something without stopping

- My Spanish class is hard, but I'm going to **keep on** going to the class.
- The teacher came into the room, but the students **kept on** talking.

#104: MAKE OUT

104: be able to understand something that is hard to hear or see or understand

- Some students can't **make out** the difference between the words *teacher* and *t-shirt*.
- Whose signature is this? I can't **make out** what it says.

#105: SHUT UP

105: ask someone to or want something to be quiet; to become quiet suddenly

- I sure wish those barking dogs would **shut up**!
- When we all looked at the angry man, he finally **shut up**.

∼

ACTIVITY 3: PRACTICING IMPORTANT PHRASES

Give the phrasal verb for the meaning. Be sure to use the correct verb tense.

1. understand what he said = _____ _____ what he said
2. continue practicing the piano = _____ _____ practicing the piano
3. he suddenly became quiet = he suddenly _____ _____
4. not stop raining = _____ _____ raining
5. no one can read what the sign says = no one can _____ _____ what the sign says

~

ACTIVITY 4: USING CORRECT PREPOSITIONS

Read the sentences carefully and add the missing prepositions for each phrasal verb.

1. Our football coach told us to **keep** _____ running with the ball.
2. I cannot wait for those loud machines to **shut** _____ .
3. Can you **make** _____ this last number? Is it a 3 or an 8?
4. Sometimes the best strategy is to **shut** _____ and avoid having an argument.
5. I won't retire now because I want to **keep** _____ working for one more year.
6. He couldn't **make** _____ what the message on his phone said.

~

ACTIVITY 5: VERBS IN CONTEXT

Use the context to select the correct verb for the sentence.

1. For once, would you please (keep on, make out, shut up) and listen?
2. I can't (keep on, make out, shut up) the difference between the E and the F in this old document.
3. It looks like it might (keep on, make out, shut up) snowing for an hour or two.
4. He was angry and shouted, "Everyone, right now (keep on, make out, shut up) and listen to what the police officer is telling us!"
5. No one can (keep on, make out, shut up) that signature.

∼

ACTIVITY 6: ONLINE PRACTICE

You can practice the phrasal verbs from this lesson at

https://bit.ly/418R4gt

Here you can use *Flashcards*, *Learn*, or *Match*. You can also have more guided practice with *Q-Chat* that offers *Teach me*, *Quiz me*, and *Apply my knowledge*.

Answers for Lesson 5

Activity 1

1. c
2. b
3. c
4. a
5. a
6. a

Activity 3

1. make out
2. keep on
3. shut up
4. keep on
5. make out

Activity 4

1. on
2. up
3. out
4. up
5. on
6. out

Activity 5

1. shut up
2. make out
3. keep on
4. shut up
5. make out

LESSON 6

BRING ABOUT; STEP BACK; TURN OFF

ACTIVITY 1: CONVERSATION PRACTICE

An old log cabin

Read this conversation. Think about the meanings of the **3 new bold verbs**. Remember the meanings of the <u>underlined verbs</u> from earlier lessons. Then answer the comprehension questions.

Tour guide (Shawn): Okay, everyone, in this part of today's tour, we're going to talk about the house that you see here on the left. This is the Fuller House. Does anyone know anything about the history of this house?

Person on a tour (Molly): Shawn, I have a question.

Shawn: Yes, what is it?

Molly: When was the house built?

Shawn: In 1860, just a few years after the owners arrived here from England. Before I say anything else, would everyone please **turn off** or just silence your phones? Thank you.

Molly: How many people lived in this little house?

Shawn: Believe it or not, six people lived here.

Molly: Six people lived in that small place?

Shawn: Yes, Edward and Ann Fuller and their four children. But they did not <u>start out</u> in this house. When they first arrived in 1854, they were in a much smaller place. They didn't have any children then, but it was still very small.

Molly: Wow. It's hard to imagine a smaller place than this.

Shawn: Yes.

Molly: Do you know why the Fullers left their home in England?

Shawn: Like many others who came before them, they

believed that this city could **bring about great** changes, and this would make their lives better. In fact, they were willing to go through a lot of very difficult times to make their lives better. It was a long journey—they took a ship and then a train through Canada to get here. But even then, it was a long time before they had enough food to live on. They often <u>ran out of</u> food, especially during the winters. But, in the end, they were happy they came here, and their house and farm <u>kept on</u> growing with their family. All this land you see around you is their land. In time, the Fuller family became one of the richest in this area.

Molly: Wow.

Shawn: Please take a look around and let me know if you have any questions.

Molly: Shawn, you're really a good tour guide. Have you always been a tour guide?

Shawn: No, actually I used to teach high school history, but two years ago, I decided to **step back** from teaching, and I took a job here as a tour guide.

1. When did the Fullers live in the cabin?

   a. before 1854
   b. between 1854 and 1860
   c. after 1860

2. How many people lived in the house?

a. six

b. nine

c. eighteen

3. Why did the Fullers leave England?

   a. They wanted to live in a small house.
   b. They wanted to have a better life in a new country.
   c. We do not know from this conversation.

4. How did the Fullers travel to their new place to live?

   a. by train through Canada
   b. by ship from Canada
   c. We do not know from this conversation.

5. What happened to the Fullers during some of the winters?

   a. They did not have a place to live.
   b. They did not have enough food to eat.
   c. They wanted to move to a warmer place.

6. How many people are on tour that is led by Shawn?

   a. two
   b. ten
   c. We do not know from this conversation.

∾

ACTIVITY 2: LEARNING NEW PHRASAL VERBS

Read this information about 3 phrasal verbs. Study the example sentences carefully. To help learn them, read the example sentences aloud or write them on a sheet of paper or in a document.

#106: BRING ABOUT

106: cause something to happen

- The war **brought about** many changes in everyone's lives.
- Making one mistake at work will not **bring about** the end of the world.

#107: STEP BACK

107: stop being involved in something, often temporarily to allow time to think about it carefully before making a final decision

- We should **step back** for a moment and consider all our options.
- I like my part-time job on the weekend, but I'm going to **step back** from that job for a while.

#108: TURN OFF

108A: temporarily stop a machine or device from working; stop the power or flow

- Don't forget to **turn off** the stove when you're finished.
- Who **turned off** the TV last night?

108B: cause someone to lose interest in a thing or a person

- A lack of good manners can easily **turn off** customers.
- Unfortunately, his teaching style **turns off** a lot of students.

∽

ACTIVITY 3: PRACTICING IMPORTANT PHRASES

Give the phrasal verb for the meaning. Be sure to use the correct verb tense.

1. cut the power to the radio = _____ _____ the radio
2. cause a change to happen = _____ _____ a change
3. make some customers lose interest = _____ some customers _____
4. stop being involved for a moment = _____ _____ for a moment
5. stop the water from flowing = _____ _____ the water

∽

ACTIVITY 4: USING CORRECT PREPOSITIONS

Read the sentences carefully and add the missing prepositions for each phrasal verb.

1. Why don't you **step** _____ and think about other
   ways to solve this problem?
2. People's love of fast food **brought** _____ many
   changes in restaurants.
3. I wish I could **step** _____ from my business for a
   while, but I have to be there every day.
4. Is it really better to **turn** _____ your computer when
   you're not using it?
5. A bad attitude can easily **turn** people _____.
6. What **brought** _____ his decision to quit his job?

～

ACTIVITY 5: VERBS IN CONTEXT

Use the context to select the correct verb for the sentence.

1. The new law did not (bring about, step back, turn off)
   the results everyone had imagined.
2. One thing that businesses do that will probably (bring
   about, step back, turn off) a lot of customers is to raise
   prices.
3. I wish I could (bring about, step back, turn off) from
   my job and go away on vacation for a month.
4. Don't forget to (bring about, step back, turn off) the
   TV when you go to bed.

5. What are the best ways to (bring about, step back, turn off) a real change in our society?

~

ACTIVITY 6: ONLINE PRACTICE

You can practice the phrasal verbs from this lesson at

https://bit.ly/4hSpoU0

Here you can use *Flashcards*, *Learn*, or *Match*. You can also have more guided practice with *Q-Chat* that offers *Teach me*, *Quiz me*, and *Apply my knowledge*.

Answers for Lesson 6

Activity 1

1. c
2. a
3. b
4. a
5. b
6. c

Activity 3

1. turn off
2. bring about
3. turn (some customers) off
4. step back
5. turn off

Activity 4

1. back
2. about
3. back
4. off
5. off
6. about

Activity 5

1. bring out
2. turn off
3. step back
4. turn off
5. bring about

LESSON 7

COME ALONG; LAY DOWN; STAND OUT

ACTIVITY 1: CONVERSATION PRACTICE

A parade

Read this conversation. Think about the meanings of the **3 new bold verbs**. Remember the meanings of the <u>underlined verbs</u> from earlier lessons. Then answer the comprehension questions.

Bonnie: Hi, Carol. [*pause*] Carol. [*pause*] Carol! Over here!

Carol: Oh, good morning, Bonnie. I'm sorry that I didn't hear you <u>calling out</u> to me. (Carol looks at her phone.)

Bonnie: No problem. I'm just <u>running out</u> now to get a few things for us to eat this weekend. I'm taking my kids to the parade later today, and I wondered if all of you want to **come along**.

Carol: Oh, my kids would love that! Sorry, let me check this one message.

Bonnie: Okay.

Carol: Thanks, that sounds great! I don't think we've been to this parade before. Tell me about it

Bonnie: Well, what **stands out** in my memory from parades in the past is that this one is kind of like going back in time, like the kind of parades you see in movies. The fire trucks throw out a lot of candy to the kids, and there are several marching bands. What I really love is that the bands are really good and play songs you would recognize from the radio, and people dance!

Carol: Who dances? The people in the parade?

Bonnie: Yes, there are dancers in the parade, but everyone on the streets dances too! That's my favorite part!

Carol: Wow! It sounds really fun. How big of a parade is it?

Bonnie: It starts near campus and then turns onto Green Avenue and goes about four blocks and finishes downtown. We usually try to watch from the same place every year, right near the start.

Carol: Okay. What time do we need to leave?

Bonnie: We should leave at noon to get parked and in our spot before the parade starts, so we have almost three more hours.

Carol: Okay, well, I'm pretty tired, so I'm going to go inside and **lay down** my phone and lie down for a little while.

Bonnie: Sounds good. Don't forget to dress for the weather. There's a chance of rain, unfortunately.

Carol: Will they still have the parade if it's raining?

Bonnie: Yes, unless there's thunder and lightning.

Carol: Okay, I'll find the raincoats and boots for everyone to bring, in case in rains.

Bonnie: Okay. See you in a few hours.

1. What day of the week is it probably?

   a. Friday
   b. Wednesday
   c. We don't know from the conversation.

2. What will they see in the parade?

a. people playing musical instruments
b. fire trucks
c. people playing musical instruments and fire trucks

3. What does Bonnie like about the parade?

    a. She likes getting the candy.
    b. She likes to dance to the music.
    c. She likes to see the fire trucks.

4. What time does the parade start?

    a. at 12 pm
    b. after 12 pm
    c. at 3 pm

5. What is Carol going to do before they leave for the parade?

    a. She will find the raincoats.
    b. She will go to the market to buy food for the parade.
    c. She will sleep for a little while.

6. What happens if it starts raining?

    a. The parade will happen as planned.
    b. The parade will happen tomorrow.
    c. The parade will not happen today.

∾

ACTIVITY 2: LEARNING NEW PHRASAL VERBS

Read this information about 3 phrasal verbs. Study the example sentences carefully. To help learn them, read the example sentences aloud or write them on a sheet of paper or in a document.

#109: COME ALONG

109A: arrive or appear at a place

- The bus will **come along** in a few minutes.
- I was not unhappy at my job, but a new opportunity **came along**, so I applied for it.

109B: go somewhere with someone else

- I'm going to the store. Do you want to **come along**?
- Who **came along** with you to the football game?

109C: develop or progress

- How is your final report **coming along**?
- The vegetables in our garden are **coming along** nicely.

#110: LAY DOWN

110A: establish or strongly announce rules or laws

- Most teachers **lay down** the rules for the classroom on the first day.
- Our new boss has **laid down** some very tough guidelines for promotions.

110B: past tense of **lie down** (lie flat, usually to rest) (Note: Many native speakers mistakenly say *lay down* for present tense, instead of *lie down*. This is informal English, and you may hear some people say, "I want to lay down now," but this is not correct in formal English.)

- As soon as Ann **lay down** last night, she fell asleep.
- The cat **lay down** on the sofa and took a long nap.

110C: put something down carefully

- The workers will **lay down** new tiles in the bathroom tomorrow.
- He **laid down** the baby and then turned off the light.

#111: STAND OUT

111: be very noticeable

- With his bright red hair, Max **stands out** in a photo.
- On a map of South America, Brazil **stands out** because of its size.

∾

ACTIVITY 3: PRACTICING IMPORTANT PHRASES

Give the phrasal verb for the meaning. Be sure to use the correct verb tense.

1. travel to a place with me = _____ _____ with me
2. José put his phone on the table = José _____ _____ his phone on the table
3. How's your job search going? = How's your job search _____ _____ ?
4. your diamond ring is easy to see = your diamond ring _____ _____
5. a better opportunity appeared = a better opportunity _____ _____

∽

ACTIVITY 4: USING CORRECT PREPOSITIONS

Read the sentences carefully and add the missing prepositions for each phrasal verb.

1. When I read your paper, no big errors **stood** _____.
2. She was sleepy, so she **lay** _____ for a while. She slept for only an hour, though.
3. When we went for a walk today, Jill's dog wanted to **come** _____.
4. We use the word *outstanding* to describe work that **stands** _____.

5. It's important for a leader to **lay** _____ the rules at the very beginning.
6. Oh no! I missed my bus. Now I'll just have to wait for the next one to **come** _____.

∾

ACTIVITY 5: VERBS IN CONTEXT

Use the context to select the correct verb for the sentence.

1. It's hard for anyone to (come along, lay down, stand out) in a really large group.
2. As soon as I (come along, lay down, stand out) on the sofa, I fell asleep.
3. I think it's important to (come along, lay down, stand out) the rules of any game before the game starts.
4. The cat (come along, lay down, stand out) in its bed and went to sleep.
5. I'm going to the bank. Do you want to (come along, lay down, stand out)?

∾

ACTIVITY 6: ONLINE PRACTICE

You can practice the phrasal verbs from this lesson at

https://bit.ly/3XgnjJs

Here you can use *Flashcards*, *Learn*, or *Match*. You can also have more guided practice with *Q-Chat* that offers *Teach me*, *Quiz me*, and *Apply my knowledge*.

Answers for Lesson 7

Activity 1

1. c
2. c
3. b
4. b
5. a
6. a

Activity 3

1. come along
2. laid down
3. coming along
4. stands out
5. came along

Activity 4

1. out
2. down
3. along
4. out
5. down
6. along

Activity 5

1. stand out
2. lay down
3. lay down
4. come along
5. come along

LESSON 8

BRING DOWN; GO AROUND; PLAY OUT

ACTIVITY 1: CONVERSATION PRACTICE

Workers fixing up an apartment building

Read this conversation. Think about the meanings of the **3 new bold verbs**. Remember the meanings of the <u>underlined verbs</u> from earlier lessons. Then answer the comprehension questions.

Nicki: Hi, Gina. Hope you're doing well this morning.

Gina: Yes. I'm fine. And you?

Nicki: Good. Things are good up here on the 5th floor. Hey, if it's okay, I'd like to **bring down** some mail that was delivered to me by mistake.

Gina: Oh, I don't think that's possible because they're doing a lot of work today on the whole 2nd floor. They're <u>laying down</u> new carpeting on the hallway and stairs outside my door this morning. I don't think anyone can **go around** all the workers and get to my door right now. Can you wait until later in the day, after work, to **bring** it **down**?

Nicki: Sure. No problem. I'm glad the building owners are actually doing the work they promised to do, like the new carpeting and painting.

Gina: Me too, but I wish we had more notice of when these things are going to happen. I thought I would be able to <u>get in</u> my car this morning before they started their work, but now it seems that I can't get out for at least another hour.

Nicki: That's frustrating.

Gina: Yeah. It's a good thing I don't have any meetings at work this morning.

Nicki: It's going to be very interesting to see how all of these changes **play out**. I'm sure this means they'll be increasing our monthly fees.

Gina: Probably. But I think it also means we'll get more money if we sell our places, so that's okay with me. But, I would really like to get more information about the timing of this work. Do you want to <u>come along</u> with me to the board meeting next week to hear what they have to say?

Nikki: Yeah, I can do that. When is it?

Gina: Next Wednesday night at 6:30 pm.

Nikki: Great, I've just added it to my calendar. Okay, I'm going to go to work now. I'll **bring** the mail **down** when I get home.

Gina: Thanks!

1. Whose mail was not delivered to the right place?

   1. Nikki's
   2. Gina's
   3. We do not know from this conversation.

2. How do Nicki and Gina know each other?

   1. They work together at an apartment rental agency.
   2. They are roommates.
   3. They live in the same building.

3. Why is no one able to get in or out of Nicki's home right now?

   1. The area outside her door is being painted.
   2. The area outside her door is being carpeted.
   3. The area outside her door has papers everywhere.

4. Why did the monthly fees Nicki and Gina pay increase?

1. The fees have not increased yet.
2. The management made changes to improve the building.
3. We do not know from this conversation.

5. What is happening next Wednesday?

1. Nicki and Gina will go to a meeting.
2. Nicki and Gina will be late for work.
3. Nicki and Gina will go out for coffee.

6. When will Gina get her mail?

1. next Wednesday
2. sometime after 5:00 today
3. We do not know from this conversation.

~

ACTIVITY 2: LEARNING NEW PHRASAL VERBS

Read this information about 3 phrasal verbs. Study the example sentences carefully. To help learn them, read the example sentences aloud or write them on a sheet of paper or in a document.

#112: BRING DOWN

112A: reduce the level or amount of something

- Can the government **bring down** the price of gas?
- The clouds might help **bring down** the temperature a bit.

112B: bring something with you from a higher place to a lower place

- They should **bring down** those boxes from the attic now.
- I'll **bring** my computer **down**, and we can work here in the lobby.

#113: GO AROUND

113A: GO AROUND + VERB-ing: spend your time behaving a certain way

- At election time, candidates **go around** asking people for their votes.
- She has been **going around** telling everyone about her new car.

113B: try to avoid something like a requirement or a step

- This app says there's a lot of traffic just ahead, so I'm looking for a way to **go around**.
- I'd like to find a way to **go around** the requirement to submit this by mail.

#114: PLAY OUT

114: happen and develop

- This argument will **play out** online until the election.
- No one knows how everything will **play out** after the new law is passed.

~

ACTIVITY 3: PRACTICING IMPORTANT PHRASES

Give the phrasal verb for the meaning. Be sure to use the correct verb tense.

1. How will things develop over time? = How will things _____ _____ over time
2. avoid the construction downtown = _____ _____ the construction downtown
3. reduce the price of rent = _____ _____ the price of rent
4. spend time telling everyone about her friend running for mayor = _____ _____ telling everyone about her friend running for mayor
5. lower the cost of airline travel = _____ _____ the cost of airline travel

~

ACTIVITY 4: USING CORRECT PREPOSITIONS

Read the sentences carefully and add the missing prepositions for each phrasal verb.

1. Who knows how things will **play** _____?
2. The rain we had in the morning **brought** _____ afternoon temperatures.
3. If you **go** _____ arguing with everyone so much, they might think you have a problem.
4. If you could predict the future, you could tell us how this election will **play** _____.
5. Can you **bring** _____ holiday decorations from the attic?
6. How long did it take you to **go** _____ all of the closed roads?

~

ACTIVITY 5: VERBS IN CONTEXT

Use the context to select the correct verb for the sentence.

1. Is it possible for one company to (bring down, go around, play out) the price of milk for everyone?
2. Let's (bring down, go around, play out) the flooded roads ahead.
3. How did everything with your job (bring down, go around, play out) once you got a new job?
4. One way to (bring down, go around, play out) your fever is to take aspirin.
5. They offered me a good salary, but I asked for more money. Right now, I don't know how all of this will (bring down, go around, play out), so I may or may not take that job offer.

~

ACTIVITY 6: ONLINE PRACTICE

You can practice the phrasal verbs from this lesson at

https://bit.ly/4gTODE7

Here you can use *Flashcards*, *Learn*, or *Match*. You can also have more guided practice with *Q-Chat* that offers *Teach me*, *Quiz me*, and *Apply my knowledge*.

Answers for Lesson 8

Activity 1

1. b
2. c
3. b
4. a
5. a
6. b

Activity 3

1. play out
2. go around
3. brought down
4. go around
5. bring down

Activity 4

1. out
2. down
3. out
4. down
5. around

Activity 5

1. bring down
2. go around
3. play out
4. bring down
5. play out

LESSON 9

BREAK OUT; GET THROUGH; HOLD BACK

ACTIVITY 1: CONVERSATION PRACTICE

Two parents talking on the phone

Read this conversation. Think about the meanings of the **3 new bold verbs**. Remember the meanings of the <u>underlined</u>

verbs from earlier lessons. Then answer the comprehension questions.

Julia: Hey, how was your day?
Travis: Interesting. How was yours?
Julia: Great, so far! The trip has <u>started out</u> really well! We **got through** airport security easily this morning. And the flight was on time, and the weather here is beautiful! I think things will go well for us tomorrow at the conference.
Travis: Oh, that's good news. You must be happy.
Julia: I am, but you seem a little strange. Did something happen? What are you **holding back**?
Travis: I wish I didn't have to tell you this, but ...
Julia: What?
Travis: Something happened at school today with Connor. He's fine. He's not hurt, but he got in trouble and can't go tomorrow.
Julia: What do you mean? What happened?
Travis: Another student <u>set off</u> the fire alarm, and at some point, a fight **broke out** with maybe 15 to 20 students. It was crazy!
Julia: So what happened?
Travis: It was just bad luck that Connor was in the hallway. I saw him, and he tried to <u>go around</u> all those people, but there was just no way. He ended up in the middle of it all.
Julia: Oh no!
Travis: And the teachers who broke up the fight took everyone involved to the principal's office and punished them all.

Julia: What? Why didn't they just punish the student who set off the alarm?

Travis: That's a good question. There's a phone call scheduled with all of the parents and the principal tomorrow. It will be interesting to see how this all plays out.

Julia: What time is the call?

Travis: Noon.

Julia: Okay, I'll make sure I'm available. What is Connor doing now?

Travis: He's in his room, probably playing video games. He's not unhappy about not having to going to school tomorrow.

Julia: I'm sure. Are you going to work from home tomorrow?

Travis: Yes, and I'll make sure he does his homework and some housework while he's at home. He's not going to be on vacation tomorrow!

Julia: Good plan. I think I'll text him and see if he'll talk to me.

Travis: Okay. Talk to you tomorrow. Have a good night.

1. Why is Julia happy?

    1. Her trip is going well.
    2. Her conference is going well.
    3. Her husband is happy.

2. What is Travis holding back?

1. what happened to Connor at school
2. what happened to Julia's flight today
3. We do not know from this conversation.

3. What happened to Connor at school?

1. He set off the fire alarm.
2. He was hurt.
3. He was punished.

4. What time is the phone call with the school tomorrow?

1. 12:00 in the morning
2. 12:00 in the afternoon
3. after 12:00

5. Who will be working tomorrow?

1. only Travis
2. only Julia
3. Travis and Julia

6. What will Connor do tomorrow?

1. He will play video games.
2. He will study and help around the house.
3. He will go to school.

∾

ACTIVITY 2: LEARNING NEW PHRASAL VERBS

Read this information about 3 phrasal verbs. Study the example sentences carefully. To help learn them, read the example sentences aloud or write them on a sheet of paper or in a document.

#115: BREAK OUT

115A: to start suddenly and sometimes violently

- War between the two countries may **break out** at any minute.
- A fire **broke out** at the bakery last night.

115B: irritations appear on your skin

- When I eat peanuts, my skin **breaks out** in a rash.
- If I'm near a cat, I always **break out**.

115C: BREAK OUT OF: escape

- Is it really impossible to **break out of** that prison?
- I'm trying to **break out of** my usual routine of going to bed late.

#116: GET THROUGH

116A: GET THROUGH (WITH): finish

- It took me 45 minutes to **get through** the exam.

- What time did you **get through with** your work?

116B: GET THROUGH (TO): succeed in contacting

- I tried to call Diana, but I couldn't **get through**.
- Were you able to **get through to** anyone at the hotel?

#117: HOLD BACK

117A: prevent something from progressing or moving forward

- A lack of money will probably **hold** this project **back** from finishing.
- My limited English is **holding** me **back** at work.

117B: control carefully

- It was really hard for me to **hold back** my anger.
- The police **held back** the crowd.

~

ACTIVITY 3: PRACTICING IMPORTANT PHRASES

Give the phrasal verb for the meaning. Be sure to use the correct verb tense.

1. control your tears = _____ _____ your tears

2. be able to contact someone = ____ ____ ____ someone
3. a fire started suddenly = a fire ____ ____
4. finish a home renovation = ____ ____ ____ a home renovation
5. war began in 1914 = war ____ ____ in 1914

∾

ACTIVITY 4: USING CORRECT PREPOSITIONS

Read the sentences carefully and add the missing prepositions for each phrasal verb.

1. If I eat chocolate, my face **breaks** ____.
2. Tell us what happened. Please don't **hold** ____.
3. How did you **get** ____ ____ anyone at the airport? I tried calling all day.
4. In my opinion, Julie's lack of experience with the English language **held** her ____ .
5. Two prisoners **broke** ____ ____ jail last week.
6. When Francis **got** ____ ____ all of his work, he went for a run.

∾

ACTIVITY 5: VERBS IN CONTEXT

Use the context to select the correct verb for the sentence.

1. If I (break out, break out of, get through to, get through with, hold back) all this work early, I'll call you and maybe we can go see a movie.
2. Whenever she eats dairy products, she almost immediately (breaks out, gets through, holds back) in a rash.
3. The farm owner decided to build a new fence to (break out, get through to, get through with, hold back) his family's animals.
4. How many prisoners (broke out, broke out of, got through to, got through with, held back) that jail last night?
5. When the signal in this area is weak, it's hard to (break out, break out of, get through to, get through with, hold back) my aunt on the phone.

~

ACTIVITY 6: ONLINE PRACTICE

You can practice the phrasal verbs from this lesson at

https://bit.ly/41bb167

Here you can use *Flashcards*, *Learn*, or *Match*. You can also have more guided practice with *Q-Chat* that offers *Teach me*, *Quiz me*, and *Apply my knowledge*.

Answers for Lesson 9

Activity 1

1. a
2. a
3. c
4. b
5. c
6. b

Activity 3

1. hold back
2. get through to
3. broke out
4. get through
5. broke out

Activity 4

1. out
2. back
3. through to
4. back
5. out of
6. through

Activity 5

1. get through
2. breaks out
3. hold back
4. broke out of
5. get through to

LESSON 10
MOVE BACK; WALK OUT; WRITE DOWN

ACTIVITY 1: CONVERSATION PRACTICE

A bowl of pho soup

Read this conversation. Think about the meanings of the **3 new bold verbs**. Remember the meanings of the <u>underlined verbs</u> from earlier lessons. Then answer the comprehension questions.

Nate: Good morning.

Teresa: Hi. I'm looking for some rice noodles. I want to make some soup for a friend who is sick. Do you know what pho is?

Nate: Yes, of course I do! The first time I had pho was several years ago when I was in Vietnam. It was amazing. I'm so happy there are lots of pho places in town now.

Teresa: Me too. I love eating it, but this will be the first time for me to make it. And my partner has never had it before.

Nate: That's exciting. Are you going to make your own soup broth or buy it?

Teresa: Someday I'd like to make my own broth, but since it's my first time making this soup, I decided to use the pre-made pho broth. I found that already.

Nate: Good. You can find rice noodles in Aisle 5. Is there anything else in the recipe I can help you find?

Teresa: Maybe. I **wrote down** everything I needed on this list. Let's see. I have the chicken, the onion, - the cilantro, and the Thai basil. I think the only other thing I haven't found yet is the fish sauce. Oh, and I think I've <u>run out of</u> ginger, so I need that, too.

Nate: Oh, if you **move back** a bit, I can <u>bring down</u> a jar of fish sauce for you. Just one, right?

Teresa: Yes. Thank you.

Nate: And the fresh ginger is right next to the onions, but you know they have frozen ginger now, so that would be in the freezer section, near the vegetables. I'm not sure which kind you prefer.

Teresa: Oh, I need lemongrass too.

Nate: Right, and don't <u>hold back</u> on that! There's so much flavor in the lemongrass.

Teresa: You've been so helpful! I'm so happy I'm going to be able to **walk out** of this store with everything I need to make a great bowl of pho!

Nate: Excellent! I hope your dinner turns out great.

Teresa: Thanks, I can't wait to see how this turns out.

Nate: Happy cooking!

1. Why is Teresa in the grocery store?

   a. She is shopping for items to make soup.
   b. She is shopping for groceries for a sick friend.
   c. She is doing her weekly shopping.

2. What is pho?

   a. a kind of rice noodles
   b. American chicken noodle soup
   c. a noodle soup from Vietnam

3. Where will Teresa find the rice noodles?

   a. on a high shelf behind her
   b. in Aisle 5
   c. We do not know from this conversation.

4. Who has eaten pho before?

    a. Teresa's friend

    b. Nate

    c. Nate and Teresa

5. Where will Teresa find the fish sauce?

    a. on a high shelf behind her

    b. in Aisle 5

    c. We do not know from this conversation.

6. Which type of ginger will Teresa use in the soup?

    a. the fresh ginger near the onions

    b. the frozen ginger in the freezer section

    c. We do not know from this conversation.

~

ACTIVITY 2: LEARNING NEW PHRASAL VERBS

Read this information about 3 phrasal verbs. Study the example sentences carefully. To help learn them, read the example sentences aloud or write them on a sheet of paper or in a document.

#118: MOVE BACK

118: return to a place to live, work, or do business

- When you finish your training, do you plan to **move back** home?
- After the walls are painted, I'll **move back** into my office.

#119: WALK OUT

119: leave a place angrily because you are not satisfied with something

- When my neighbor said the fence between our yards was not a problem, I **walked out** of the neighborhood meeting.
- The movie was so bad that I **walked out** after only 20 minutes.

#120: WRITE DOWN

120: put words or notes on paper

- She forgot to **write down** her new password.
- Sometimes it's hard to know what is important to **write down** during a lecture.

∽

ACTIVITY 3: PRACTICING IMPORTANT PHRASES

Give the phrasal verb for the meaning. Be sure to use the correct verb tense.

1. make a note about a phone number = _____ _____ a phone number
2. return to your old office = _____ _____ to your old office
3. leave a meeting angrily = _____ _____ of a meeting
4. start to live in your hometown again = _____ _____ to your hometown
5. put your grocery list on paper = _____ _____ your grocery list

∾

ACTIVITY 4: USING CORRECT PREPOSITIONS

Read the sentences carefully and add the missing prepositions for each phrasal verb.

1. Oh, no! I forgot to **write** _____ mayonnaise and mustard on my shopping list.
2. You **walked** _____ of the movie early and didn't see the surprise ending.
3. This weekend I plan to help Joshua **move** _____ into his old place.
4. There were so many arguments during that city council meeting that I had to **walk** _____.
5. Good students try to **write** _____ all the important things the professor says.
6. If I return to my hometown, it'll be like **moving** _____ to my life of 30 years ago.

∾

ACTIVITY 5: VERBS IN CONTEXT

Use the context to select the correct verb for the sentence.

1. Are you thinking of (moving back, walking out, writing down) to Colombia?
2. I can't remember the address, and I didn't (move it back, walk it out, write it down).
3. If the meeting doesn't go as I hope, I might (move back, walk out, write down).
4. If I (move back, walk out, write down) into my old apartment, the rent will be cheaper than my current place.
5. Please (move back, walk out, write down) all the things you want me to buy at the store.

∽

ACTIVITY 6: ONLINE PRACTICE

You can practice the phrasal verbs from this lesson at

https://bit.ly/4if5Rx7

Here you can use *Flashcards*, *Learn*, or *Match*. You can also have more guided practice with *Q-Chat* that offers *Teach me*, *Quiz me*, and *Apply my knowledge*.

Answers for Lesson 10

Activity 1

1. a
2. c
3. b
4. c
5. a
6. c

Activity 3

1. write down
2. move back
3. walk out
4. move back
5. write down

Activity 4

1. down
2. out
3. back
4. out
5. down
6. back

Activity 5

1. moving back
2. write it down
3. walk out
4. move back
5. write down

ABOUT THE PUBLISHER

Thank you for your time and attention! If you found the book useful, we hope you will leave a short review on the site where you purchased this book to let other readers know of your experience.

To be notified about new titles and special contests, events, and sales from Wayzgoose Press, please visit our website at

http://wayzgoosepress.com

and sign up for our mailing list. (We send email infrequently, and you can unsubscribe at any time.)

~